My Little Book of Everyday Prayers

Written and compiled by
Felicity Henderson

Illustrations by
Toni Goffe

A LION BOOK

Oxford . Batavia . Sydney

Today

This is the day
that God has made.
We will rejoice and
be glad in it.

Father, we thank you

Father, we thank you for the night,
And for the pleasant morning light;
For rest and food and loving care,
And all that makes the day so fair.
Help us to do the things we should,
To be to others kind and good;
In all we do at work or play
To grow more loving every day.

Shopping

We went shopping today.
Mom bought me a pair of new, red boots.
Thank you, God, for my shiny, red boots.

Thank you for our food

Thank you, God, for our food.
Thank you for my favorites —
hot dogs and ice-cream.
Help us to help other people
who haven't got enough to eat.

At my house

At my house,
I like sitting in my special chair
reading my books,
or playing with my toys.
I like it at my house.
Thank you, God, for my house.

Nursery school

Dear God, I like nursery school.
There's water and sand
and books and toys.
There's painting and dressing-up.
Can I go again tomorrow?

Feeding the ducks

I'm glad you made ducks.
I like feeding them.
Thank you, God.

Jesus, may I be like you

Jesus, may I be like you;
Loving, kind in all I do;
Kind and happy when I play
Close beside you all the day.

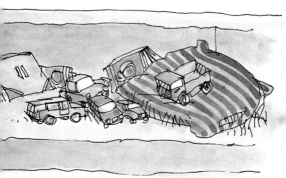

All things bright and beautiful

All things bright and beautiful,
All creatures great and small,
All things wise and wonderful
The Lord God made them all.

Two little eyes

Two little eyes to look to God;
Two little ears to hear his word;
Two little feet to walk in his ways;
Two little lips to sing his praise;
Two little hands to do his will
And one little heart to love him still.

Playing outdoors

Let's go on the see-saw,
Then up and down the slide.
We can climb the jungle gym
And swing from side to side.
I like playing outdoors.
Thank you, God.

Helping at our house

Today I helped Mom at our house.
It was fun.
We made cookies and I
washed the dishes.
Thank you, God, for today.

A blessing

May the love of God our Father
Be in all our homes today:
May the love of the Lord Jesus
Keep our hearts and minds always:
May his loving Holy Spirit
Guide and bless the ones I love,
Father, mother, brothers, sisters,
Keep them safely in his love.

Text copyright © 1988 Lion Publishing
Illustrations copyright © 1988 Toni Goffe

Published by
Lion Publishing plc
Sandy Lane West, Oxford, England
ISBN 0 7459 1251 6
Lion Publishing Corporation
1705 Hubbard Avenue, Batavia, Illinois 60510, USA
ISBN 0 7459 1251 6
Albatross Books Pty Ltd
PO Box 320, Sutherland, NSW 2232, Australia
ISBN 0 86760 940 0

First edition 1988
Reprinted 1988, 1989, 1990 (twice), 1991 (three times)

Acknowledgments
Copyright prayers as follows:
'Jesus, may I be like you' from *Hymns and
Songs for Children*, National Society; 'Two little eyes'
from *CSSM Chorus Book I*, Scripture Union;
'May the love of God our Father' from *Infant Prayer*,
Oxford University Press

Printed and bound in Singapore